W9-DGF-434

DOROTHY HOLE

# THE NAVY AND YOU

CRESTWOOD HOUSE
NEW YORK
MAXWELL MACMILLAN CANADA
TORONTO
MAXWELL MACMILLAN INTERNATIONAL
NEW YORK • OXFORD • SINGAPORE • SYDNEY

## DEDICATION

*For my husband, Mac L. Hole, who served during World War II*
*with the United States Navy in the Middle East*

Photo Credits: *All photos courtesy of the United States Navy.*

*Cover design, text design and production: William E. Frost Associates Ltd.*

*Library of Congress Cataloging-in-Publication Data*

Hole, Dorothy.
  The navy and you / by Dorothy Hole. —1st ed.
    p.  cm. — (The armed forces)
  Summary: Discusses navy life in detail and lists the
advantages and disadvantages to consider before joining this
branch of the armed forces.
  ISBN 0-89686-767-6
  1. United States.  Navy — Vocational guidance — Juvenile
literature. [1. United States. Navy — Vocational guidance.
2. Vocational guidance.]  I. Title. II. Series: Hole, Dorothy.
Armed forces.
VB259.H65 1993
359'.0023'73 — dc20                                    92-9055

CRESTWOOD HOUSE                MAXWELL MACMILLAN CANADA, INC.
MACMILLAN PUBLISHING COMPANY        1200 Eglinton Avenue East
866 Third Avenue                            Suite 200
New York, NY 10022              Don Mills, Ontario M3C 3N1

*Macmillan Publishing Company is part of the*
*Maxwell Communication Group of Companies*
*First Edition*
*Printed in the United States of America*

10  9  8  7  6  5  4  3  2  1

# CONTENTS

# CHAPTER ONE

# THINKING IT OVER

One day your buddy says, "Let's join the navy."

"Join the navy!" you say. "Why?"

"Lots of reasons," your friend continues. "Steady job, regular paycheck, travel"—there's a pause—"and adventure!"

Sounds exciting, you think. You picture yourself in a sailor's uniform, standing on the deck of a **cruiser**, the wind in your face and clean, fresh air in your lungs.

The scene changes. Still in uniform, you're surrounded by Italians as your picture is taken with you standing in front of a Roman fountain. Or perhaps you're in Egypt, posing beside the pyramids. Or in Japan, shopping for presents.

But there must be more to the navy than adventure and sightseeing! You're right, there is.

A navy **recruiter** can answer your questions about length of enlistment, job opportunities, housing, medical benefits and

*(Photo left)   As a member of the United States Navy, you might get the chance to experience life at sea, while serving aboard an aircraft carrier like this one.*

whether or not you have to know how to swim. But the real place to start is with *you*.

It's *your* life, *your* future, and you need to be sure that the navy offers a lifestyle that you want.

Begin with the things that you might not like. Be honest with yourself. Ask, "Will I adjust to sleeping in a bunk? What if the **seaman** in the upper bunk snores? Will that keep me awake? How will I handle that? And living with all those strangers on a small ship? Will I like it?"

Then there are the separations from family and friends. Balance that against your interest in seeing the world. Will you be homesick? Have you ever been away from home for long periods? It's something to think about.

Most seamen are on a sea-shore rotation. That means you spend three years on shore for every four years in a sea command. Although not all four years are spent at sea, you will have times when your ship will **deploy**, or leave its home port. This normally lasts six months, although not every day is spent sailing.

You must obey orders. Does that come easily or do you rebel against being told what to do? You may begin to feel like a robot. In the navy a sailor never asks, "Why?", never says, "I don't feel like it" or "I'll do it later." You are treated like an adult and must act like one.

A small ship (a **frigate** or a **destroyer escort**) is where you want to serve. Instead, you're ordered to a battleship and are just one seaman among many. The largest type of warship, a Nimitz class aircraft **carrier**, has a crew of almost 6,000.

With all those people, what chance is there for privacy? Hey, do sailors get seasick?

How well do you face danger? Perhaps you never have and don't know the answer. In peacetime there is no more risk for a seaman than for a civilian doing the same job. In wartime that is not true. Naval vessels, at sea or in port, are always enemy targets.

After a while you may feel that you've lost control of your life. Others, mostly unknown to you, decide where you'll go, what you'll eat, what you'll do and when you'll sleep. It's not a matter of trying navy life for a few months and then quitting if you don't like it. When you join, you sign a legally binding contract. All you can do is wait it out until your enlistment years are up.

If this seems overwhelming, forget the navy. It's not for you.

"Wait a minute," you say. "Many young men and women do enlist in the navy. With all these negative reasons, what convinces them? Why do some reenlist?'

The recruiter can tell you, but before you head toward the recruiting station, talk to your school counselor.

*This young man has learned to read and understand a weather map while serving in the navy. This valuable skill can lead to a career in the field of meteorology in civilian life.*

# CHAPTER TWO

# LEARNING MORE ABOUT YOU

Your school counselor tells you that before you enlist in the navy, you must take a test, the **Armed Services Vocational Aptitude Battery (ASVAB)**.

The ASVAB helps you—and the navy—learn more about you. You discover your abilities, your skills and your talents (you may be surprised!). This test guides the navy in placing you in a job skill that interests you and that you want and can successfully do.

In the navy or out, you can use the ASVAB. It shows you what jobs to apply for in civilian life. You may have ability in more skills than you realize.

This test is taken by applicants for all the armed services. Many subjects are included. There are math, general science,

*(Photo left)   The navy is made up of men and women who take pride in representing their country.*

word knowledge and auto and shop information questions, among others.

A sample auto question:

"A car uses too much oil when which parts are worn?

    A. Pistons

    B. Piston rings

    C. Main bearings

    D. Connecting rod"

Know the answer?

If you're worried about flunking, go to the library. You will find books especially written to help you pass the ASVAB. Study them. Take sample tests. Learn from your wrong answers.

Discuss your score with a recruiter. Some schools ask a recruiter to explain the scores. This will give you a better idea of how the navy feels about you.

Don't despair if you flunk! Wait 30 days and take it again. After that, six months must go by before you can try once more.

You decide to talk to a recruiter. Where do you find one? Look in the telephone directory under "United States Government, Navy Recruiting." Make a list of questions and then pay the recruiter a visit.

*The navy has many job opportunities and programs to choose from, both on land and at sea.*

First, the recruiter tells you that both men and women, single or married, may enlist, unless they are a single parent with child custody. If that's the case, the navy will not accept you.

Between your 17th and your 35th birthdays, you're eligible. Before you turn 18, you need the consent of a parent or guardian. After you turn 35, you will not be accepted.

If you are a United States citizen, proof of citizenship is required (usually your birth certificate will do). Legal papers proving citizenship are especially important if you were born outside the United States.

If you are not a citizen, you must show that you entered the country legally as a permanent resident (a green card). Also bring along your social security card and driver's license.

The navy prefers you graduate from high school, although it is not a must. Many courses are offered by the navy, so you might get your diploma after enlisting.

"How long do I have to stay in the navy?" you ask. It's up to you: three, four, five or six years. However, the navy enlistment program you pick may have a minimum time requirement.

One word of warning: Be absolutely honest in what you tell the navy. If you have a drug or alcohol problem, say so. If you've been on drugs, the navy will turn you down. If you've been arrested, say so. The navy will find out anyway, so don't lie.

The recruiter recites the benefits: a 30-day paid vacation each year, free meals and housing, medical and dental care, entertainment—movies, gyms, libraries, TVs, even golf courses and campgrounds—some on shipboard, some (as you've guessed!) not. Some are free; some cost a small amount. If you want to continue your education, no matter where you're stationed, on land or sea, you can do it. The recruiter tells you how.

What you really want to know is, "What job will I do in the navy? Do I have a choice?"

These navy crew members are monitoring consoles at their dive
stations in the control room of a nuclear-powered submarine.

# CHAPTER THREE

# WHAT TYPES OF JOBS ARE AVAILABLE IN THE NAVY?

A wide variety of jobs are necessary to keep the navy's ships afloat, planes in the air and **submarines** under the ocean's surface.

More than 100 career skills, each covering many jobs, are open for you to choose from. What'll it be: barber, data control, hospital corpsman, cook, weapons technician or torpedoman? Keep in mind that whatever you do in the navy, there is a civilian job using the same skill.

"Torpedoman?" you question.

Electronics is the answer.

Yes, you do have a choice. Whether or not the navy agrees with you on what job you can do successfully depends on the results of your ASVAB and interviews with the recruiter and navy guidance counselor. A computer matches your skills with job vacancies.

You have no special interests or skills? Consider the Seaman/Airman/Fireman **Apprenticeship Program**. As a seaman, when you finish your training, you'll probably serve on a ship. If you're a woman, you can sign on as a seaman but you will not be guaranteed a ship assignment. The number of seagoing assignments for women is limited.

The Congress of the United States passed a law in the summer of 1991 that now permits women in combat areas. This opens up more shipboard jobs for women.

If you pick airman, you learn everything about aircraft from structural repair to electronics. However, enlisted personnel cannot be pilots except on helicopters.

The remaining apprenticeship—**fireman**—is not a fire fighter. This **recruit** trains to become an engineman, machinery repairman or gas turbine systems technician.

Seamen and firemen can choose on which coast they wish to serve. The needs of the navy come first. Although you've been guaranteed duty where you want to be, it may not happen.

Once again, there are limited assignments for women in the apprenticeship program. If you are a woman, you will not have a choice of coast.

"Hey," you say, "I know exactly what I want to do —be an electrician (or boiler technician or machinist's mate)."

In that case, if you qualify, after recruit training you go to a **Class "A" specialist school**. These are located wherever the navy has facilities, such as Norfolk, Virginia, or San Diego, California.

---

*(Photo right)   This recruit is training to be a disbursing clerk, a skill that may be useful to him in almost any career he chooses in civilian life.*

If you become a construction electrician, you do mechanical and electrical work. In civilian life the field is wide open for someone with that background.

You're interested in office work. How about being a disbursing clerk? You'll keep military pay records, prepare payroll and write reports—the same duties needed by every corporation in America.

If you wonder why water comes out of a faucet when you turn the handle, sign on as a utilities man. You'll be responsible for plumbing, heating and waste disposal plus water purification units.

Although the recruiter matches your skills and interests with navy job openings, the final decision is made at the **Military Entrance Processing Station (MEPS)**.

If there are no vacancies in your choice, you'll be in the **Delayed Entry Program**. This places you in the **inactive reserve**. This puts off your reporting for **active service** until an opening occurs. You have the chance to finish high school or earn extra money. It may last as long as a year.

You've made up your mind to enlist. The recruiter asks you to fill in and sign an application form. It is *not* an enlistment contract.

You can still change your mind. It also means that the navy does *not* have to accept you. You find out if you qualify at the MEPS.

You must show up early in the morning. The MEPS desk opens at 5:30 A.M. If you live many miles away the navy pays for your transportation and for your hotel room the night before you report.

The morning will be spent in exams and interviews. If you've not yet taken the ASVAB, now is the time. If you have, then you'll probably begin with a physical given by a Department of Defense doctor. Tell him of any surgery, broken bones

As a boiler technician, this recruit was given the opportunity to assist in the main engine room aboard an aircraft carrier used in Operation Desert Storm.

or serious illnesses you have had. If possible, bring copies of your own doctor's records.

You will be tested for alcohol and drug abuse during your physical exam. A small amount of blood is taken to test you for HIV, the virus that causes AIDS. Your eyes are checked. Do you need glasses? Are you color-blind? These conditions will not keep you out, but the navy wants to know.

Are you under four feet ten inches or over six feet six inches? If so, the navy cannot accept you.

Then comes the **Entrance National Agency Checks (ENTNAC)** interview. The interviewer makes sure you are not a security risk to the country. Your fingerprints will be taken, sent to the FBI and kept with your naval records.

You're getting hungry. Lunch in the MEPS dining room is free. If you go outside the building to eat, you have to pay for your meal.

Now comes the most important interview: matching your skills and interests to job vacancies. A guidance counselor discusses your options.

The apprentice program is a popular one but there are others for you to consider. Some are limited to men. The Divefarer Program sounds exciting. This includes the **Special Warfare Sea, Air and Land (SEAL)** Program. You can see yourself dressed in a wet suit, slipping over the side of a rubber boat and swimming toward enemy installations on shore. To qualify, you not only have to be a man, you have to pass tough physical training. **Boot camp** is a breeze compared to this! There is also the Explosive Ordnance Program (EOP) and the Navy Diver Program. **Ordnance** means "bombs."

The navy is strong on high-tech equipment. For those more studious, there is special training in the nuclear field, advanced electronics and advanced technical field. To pick

*If you qualify, you can receive special training on the high-tech equipment used in the United States Navy.*

these areas, you must enlist for six years. The guidance counselor will tell you if you qualify.

The navy is like a large corporation with hundreds of jobs. It's just a matter of determining what you want to do and what the navy decides you can do and making them match.

If you find you're in the wrong job skill, you can change to another. The navy encourages you to "stretch out" for advanced training.

Once you, the guidance counselor and the computer agree, you sign the enlistment contract. This is a legally binding contract. READ IT CAREFULLY! You don't want to find yourself a cook instead of a fireman because you were so nervous you didn't read the contract correctly. Take your time!

Now that this is settled, you have your picture taken for identification. Then comes the swearing-in ceremony.

"I solemnly swear," you repeat, ending with, "So help me God."

You are now in the navy!

*During boot camp, you will learn the meaning and importance of teamwork.*

# CHAPTER FOUR

# THE BEGINNING

Soon you're on your way to boot camp (recruit training). A few days after you're sworn in, you report to the MEPS. The navy arranges transportation from there to the **Naval Training Center (NTC).**

This is not true, of course, if you enlisted under the Delayed Entry Program. In that case, you await orders until there is an opening in your chosen skill.

If you are a woman, you go to Orlando, Florida, the only NTC for women. For a man, it's one of three: Orlando; Great Lakes, Illinois; or San Diego, California.

"What should I take with me?" you ask. "Underwear, deodorant, washcloths, or does the navy issue those?"

Don't bring them. You buy them at the **Navy Exchange**, or **post exchange**.

"Do I pay for them with cash?"

When you arrive, you receive a coupon book, called a **chit book**, worth between $75 and $100. The coupons are your money at the Navy Exchange.

When you finish boot camp, you're paid for any coupons you haven't used. Bring no more than $25 cash with you.

Before reporting for active duty, you receive the following lists to guide you in what to bring:

1. Legal papers and medication. *Most important: Bring your social security card.*
2. Items you need if you arrive on a Friday or Saturday—two of each: slacks or jeans, shirts or blouses, clean underwear, clean socks.
3. Optional items, including cash, a light sweater or, in winter, a jacket, at least six postage stamps and, for women, a swimsuit (conservative, no low front or side cuts).

If you're a woman, you get another list. This includes such items as panty hose, bras, slips and, if your doctor prescribed them, birth control pills. Tank tops, halter tops and shorts are a definite *no!*

"Can I bring my radio or camera? I play the tuba (or saxophone or guitar). Can I bring it?"

No. You have to use your memory, not photos, to recall boot camp. And there is no time for tuba playing.

"May I bring my favorite perfume?"

Leave it home, along with your radio, tape recorder, football and jewelry. Only a small religious medal, engagement and wedding rings and a basic watch are permitted.

There are 11 categories of forbidden items, and 25 other items you purchase at the Navy Exchange. Remember, no

*Recruit training will probably put you in better physical shape than you've ever been in before.*

sharp points. Nail scissors, no; nail clippers, yes. When you get your **Bluejackets'** Manual, you feel you're really a sailor!

Almost immediately, you are given your uniform and other clothing. There is no insignia on the sleeve. Your **rating** (rank) is Seaman Recruit. Those crazy-looking things are leggings, called **boots** in navy talk. Only recruits wear them. That's why recruit training is known as boot camp.

At NTC you are part of a **Recruit Training Command (RTC)**. Eighty new recruits make up a company, which is given a number and a flag, called a **guidon** (pronounced guide-on). You and the others clean the **barracks** (building that is your home away from home) and undergo drill, dress, locker and barracks inspections together.

Your first night at recruit training is a lonely and scary one. You wonder if you've made a mistake. You wish you were home in your own bed. Just remember, you are not alone. Probably everyone in your barracks is feeling the same way.

During the eight weeks of recruit training, these strangers become your closest friends. You learn to work as a team. You suffer together through physical training and academic tests. Almost every minute of the day and night, you're with each other.

The first days are spent meeting your company commanders (CCs), who are chief petty **officers** and petty officers (enlisted men with higher rank). They are the ones who are tough on you and never satisfied with how well you do, especially in physical training.

They want you to be in the best condition possible. They know that in time of war or an emergency, what they teach you may save your life. You think that they don't know how exhausted you are. You're ready to drop. Then you hear, "Ten more push-ups." They yell at you and may even call you names! Keep in mind there's a reason for what they make you do.

But if you rebel, if your temper flares out of control, if you yell back—forget the navy!

As a woman, in the final test you must do 24 push-ups in two minutes. If you're a man, the number of push-ups in the same two minutes is 51. A woman needs to run 1.5 miles in 15 minutes; a man in 11 minutes.

Yes, by the time you finish, you must be able to swim. For that, men and women have the same requirements: Enter feet first from five feet above the water, float or tread for five minutes, then swim one lap of a 50-meter pool.

"I'll never make it!" you moan.

Here's a hint: Ask your recruiter for a booklet describing an eight-week recommended exercise program for you to follow *before* you report for duty. If you do the exercises, you'll be in good physical condition and have no trouble. No promises that your muscles won't ache!

*Both men and women are required to take part in the navy's Recruit Training Command.*

# CHAPTER FIVE

# A NEW WAY OF LIFE

Everything seems strange to you—even seeing yourself in the mirror! A man's hair is cut too short to comb. A woman's is cut so that, when combed straight, it's higher than her uniform's collar.

You'd probably be happier, if you're a woman, having your hair styled before you leave for RTC, although there is a hair salon in Orlando. Also, you only wear makeup when an official photograph is taken, on pass-in-review day and when on **liberty**.

Part of your bewilderment comes from navy lingo. It's almost like a foreign language. Some of the words you may know. "Liberty" means you have permission to leave the base, usually for only 48 hours. "Leave" is a longer vacation.

*(Photo left)   Women—if you've decided that navy life is for you, be prepared to have your hair cut so that it clears your collar.*

Soon you'll call a wall a **bulkhead**, the ceiling **overhead**, stairs a **ladder**, a bunk a **rack** and candy, gum and the cafeteria **geedunk**. Ranks are referred to as ratings, which also includes your specialty (BT2 means boiler technician second class). You'll even know what DDPO, MAA and NQS mean (division duty petty officer, master-at-arms and nonqualified swimmer).

Dinner is at 1700. Didn't anyone tell the navy the clock only goes to 12? You learn the navy counts hours up to 24. Midnight is 2400, so that means dinner is at 5 P.M. civilian time.

Your day begins at 0530. From then until **taps** (lights out) at 2130, you're busy every moment. From **reveille** (get-up time) until 0720, you clean the barracks and have breakfast and physical training.

The day is divided into ten training periods, starting at 0720 and ending at dinnertime. The only break is the 40-minute lunch period. The three hours after dinner are occupied with showers, shining shoes, cleaning the barracks (again!), studying, writing letters, receiving instructions from the RCPO (recruit chief petty officer) and a night bunk check.

You're not allowed incoming telephone calls. Within 48 to 72 hours after arrival, you call home. After that, there's a chance you may make a collect call one evening or weekend.

You spend 85 percent of the day in classrooms studying some 41 subjects. You learn about ships and aircraft, survival at sea, CBR (chemical, biological, radiological) warfare/defense, damage control, maritime threat, small arms, education benefits, antiterrorism, basic deck seamanship, conduct ashore, navy regulation, navy history and much more.

You discover why John Paul Jones is the first American naval hero and how his brilliant seamanship played such a

*(Photo right)   Your recruit chief petty officer will probably be the person who is toughest on you during training.*

28

large part in the colonists winning independence from Britain during the American Revolution. You learn that the first women to serve in the navy were recruited in 1917 to replace men who went to fight in World War I. And you're told that the official surrender of Japan in World War II took place on a naval ship, the USS *Missouri.*

By the first day of the fifth week, you have to know the 11 **General Orders** for standing watch. Anytime, anywhere, by anyone, you can be ordered to recite from memory all 11 or any specific one. Examples:

1. To take charge of this post and all government property in view
3. To report all violations of orders I am instructed to enforce
7. To talk to no one except in the line of duty

The most important part of navy life is obeying orders. You learn to obey automatically. In an emergency your acting quickly may save lives, including your own.

With flags flying on Graduation Day, you proudly march with your company before family and friends. You're finished with boots—and boot camp!

When you signed on, which did you choose, apprentice-ship or Class "A" school?

Apprentice seamen/airmen/firemen stay on at the RTC for three to four weeks for hands-on training. Then you're ordered to **the Fleet** for on-the-job training. This lasts another four weeks. Then you receive your orders.

If you become interested in a technical specialty and want to switch to it, you can work toward a transfer to a Class "A" school. Whether or not you are transferred depends on a lot of things, such as how well you're doing in your current assignment, length of time before your enlistment is up (you can reenlist, of course) and your commander's approval.

Those who chose a specialty when they enlisted go directly to Class "A" schools after boot camp. Length of training varies. This is where you practice your skills. As a damage controller, you must know how to identify the source of a fire and how to fight it. You practice fighting real fires. As a machinery repairman, you demonstrate you know how to overhaul ships' engines.

Now you're ready for your first **tour of duty** (the term for length of assignment).

If you're assigned to shore duty, you serve wherever there is a naval facility, in the United States or overseas. This could be at an air station, naval base, technical school or command headquarters. You might even have duty at an American embassy.

Most navy bases have everything you need, including housing, markets (**commissaries**), movie theaters, recreational facilities and medical offices.

If you're married, you will probably live off the base and receive a special allowance to help pay your expenses. You go to work in the morning and come home at night, just like a civilian. And just like a civilian, you may work some nights.

But you know at any moment you can be ordered to the Fleet—and then everything changes.

# CHAPTER SIX

# LIFE AT SEA

For those assigned to the Fleet, life is very different. When at sea, the ship keeps going 24 hours. Seamen don't lock the door and go home for dinner. That doesn't mean you don't sleep, eat and have free time.

The type of ship you're assigned to determines the quality of your life. On a new ship like a carrier, your bunk is large, with its own light, air-conditioning vent and fire-resistant curtains to give you privacy.

On older ships, you sleep in a large room with stacked bunks, each one 32 inches wide. Forget privacy.

The sailor in the bunk above snores? Don't worry, there are so many other noises the snoring will be drowned out. On a

---

*(Photo left)* Life at sea can be dangerous, especially during wartime, when naval vessels become major enemy targets.

carrier, it is noisy under the flight deck—and your rack might be there.

Other ships have engines and equipment that make a racket. Longtime sailors claim that after the first week, you won't hear the noise. If you're a light sleeper, you have to decide if you want to risk not sleeping well.

On some ships, the food is delicious. On others, it is so bad that hamburgers are called "sliders" because they're so greasy they slide down your throat!

How do you spend your free time? It varies as much as the comfort of the bunks. It's possible to jog around the flight deck of a carrier, and pushing planes to one side leaves space for a basketball court.

Almost all ships hold occasional "steel beach picnics" (barbecues). A 55-gallon metal drum is cut in half; on a grill over the open top, meat is cooked. Smaller ships sometimes use the helicopter pad for barbecues.

The age of your ship has a lot to do with the living and recreational facilities. Your ship may show movies and have closed-circuit TV, a library and a snack shop, but the navy doesn't promise.

Another way of spending free time is to study. "No way," you say. Think about it. It could lead to promotion, and the navy makes sure you get your education even when at sea. One program, **Program for Afloat College Education (PACE)**, offers courses that are freshman and sophomore college level. On many ships, your instructor travels with you.

Some ships are floating factories where you may be repairing equipment or even working in a foundry. Men and women work side by side.

This has given the navy a new and very serious problem. On smaller ships, what to do with free time is very limited. Weight lifting, reading and watching TV are about all there is.

The navy has issued strict **fraternization** orders, regulating physical contact between the sexes. Don't be intimate! During six months at sea or in foreign ports, you can be lonesome and find comfort in a sailor of the opposite sex. This frequently leads to pregnancy.

A pregnant sailor means the loss of a trained worker. The navy spends a lot of time and money training you. The sailor's health may be in danger because of the work she does. She is quickly transferred to shore duty. After a six-week maternity leave, she is expected to return to active service. Four months later she is up for shipboard assignment. Because of this, many women ask for a discharge. They usually get their request.

When your ship is deployed for six months, you are not sailing continuously. On one Western Pacific deployment, the longest a carrier was at sea was 19 days; the fewest in port, three days; the most, ten. After the workday, about one-quarter or one-fifth of the crew stay on board while the rest have liberty. This gives you a chance to play tourist in other countries. Of course, it's not a vacation; you can't pick what ports or for how long!

"Nineteen days at sea!" you exclaim. "What if I get seasick?"

The navy has had long experience with seasick sailors. They have cures. The ship's doctor will take care of you.

The navy is a working organization. Playing basketball, watching TV or jogging, you are still on a warship or a support ship. One of the navy's purposes is to preserve peace. However, if war breaks out, you are an enemy target.

# CHAPTER SEVEN

# RATINGS AND PAY

"How often do I get paid?" you ask.

Twice a month, except during recruit training. Then you get paid two or three times, depending on which RTC you attend. When you finish training, you get paid up to date, less any coupons you spent from your chit book and for your **ditty bag** (laundry bag).

"When do I get an increase in pay?"

When you move from your current rating to a higher one, your pay increases with your rating. One of the first things you learn to recognize during recruit training is the insignia on

*(Photo left)   As you move up in rank after recruit training, your pay, as well as the insignia on your sleeve, will change.*

37

other uniforms—especially those you must salute. You always salute an officer!

As a seaman recruit (**E-1**), you have no insignia. At the end of nine months, you can become a seaman apprentice (**E-2**). This promotion depends on your commanding officer's approval. Now you have a patch on your sleeve: a rectangle with two diagonal white stripes.

To move up and replace the two white stripes with three, you must fill the time requirements for being a seaman apprentice. You must also have done good work, pass an examination in your skill and have the okay of your commanding officer. You are now a seaman (**E-3**).

The next higher rating makes you a **noncommissioned officer**, a petty officer third class (**E-4**). Your new patch has a spread-winged eagle. Under the eagle is an emblem showing your specialty. Under that are red chevrons, one for E-4, two for petty officer second class, three for petty officer first class. After that, the design of the chevrons changes. A star appears above the eagle of the senior chief petty officer (**E-8**) and the number of stars increases until three appear on the patch of master chief of the navy (**E-9**). That is the highest rating for an enlisted sailor.

Don't let it worry you. You learn them quickly.

If you are not sure you want to commit yourself for three years, you should consider the Naval Reserve.

The three programs offered for you in the Naval Reserve are

1. **Training and Administration of Reserves (TAR)**
2. **Active Mariner Program**
3. **Sea/Air/Mariner Program (SAM)**

*(Photo right)   The skills taught in the Naval Reserve are similar to those of the regular navy.*

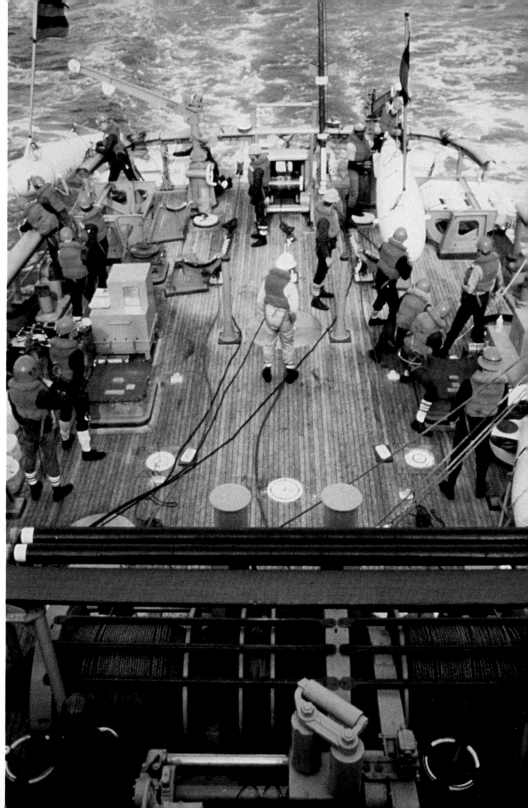

Entrance requirements are the same for the reserves as for the regular navy. You must be 17 years old and under 35, enlist for eight years and have the same proof of citizenship or a green card.

Under all these programs, you are on active duty for a specified time. You learn navy skills that may help you in the civilian work force. You are paid for your active duty time.

Under the TAR program, you serve four years active duty. Then you can reenlist for another four years active service or be transferred to the Ready Reserve for the remaining four years of your enlistment contract.

In the Active Mariner Program, your three-year active duty is followed by a three-year Selected Reserve period of drilling and additional training with a local reserve unit.

The SAM program offers recruit training during summer vacation if you are still in school. This is part of the four to six months of active duty you've agreed to serve. After that, you serve with your local reserve unit.

As an inactive reservist waiting for your eight-year enlistment to be up, you can be called into active service. This caught many inactive reservists by surprise when the Persian Gulf conflict occurred. They forgot they still had time left under their enlistment contract.

# CHAPTER EIGHT

# PASS-IN-REVIEW

Sounds almost too good to be true, doesn't it? Review the excellent benefits: 30-day paid vacation each year, choice of job (if there's an opening), learning or switching to a second skill if you're not happy with the first, forming friendships, opportunity for education, travel, free housing and, after 20 years, good retirement pay.

Reconsider. You have little control over your life. You'll be separated from your family for long periods. You have to do what you're ordered to do without questioning it. You feel that you have lost your individualism. If you're a man, how about

*If it's excitement you're looking for, the navy has plenty to offer. This navy skydiver is having fun while learning a valuable skill.*

six months on a carrier with 6,000 men and no women? If you're a woman, how about being one of very few females in a mostly male crew? Do you have the savvy to know how to be friendly without letting your coworkers think you want to continue the friendship after work hours?

Keep in mind that even if you enlist for three years, you are actually signing up for eight. You can be called back into active duty at any moment.

It all boils down to *you* and how you would react to navy life. Some people dislike it and look forward to getting out. Some people love it and reenlist time after time. Some believe it's a wonderful experience. Many bluejackets feel pride in being part of the United States Navy.

This overview of navy life may help you decide.

*If you've decided to enlist in the navy or the Naval Reserve based on the benefits and opportunities offered, keep in mind that as a bluejacket, you can encounter conflict at any time. If this frightens you, you may want to reconsider.*

# GLOSSARY

**Active Mariner Program**  One of the programs for serving in the Naval Reserve.

**active service**  The navy is your only job. You are a full-time sailor.

**Apprenticeship Program**  A program in which a new recruit receives training as an airman, seaman or fireman.

**Armed Services Vocational Aptitude Battery (ASVAB)**  A test required of all those who hope to join one of the armed services.

**barracks**  Building in which you sleep and keep your belongings.

**bluejacket**  Nickname for an enlisted man or woman in the navy.

**boot camp**  Your first training (basic training) after reporting for duty at a Naval Training Center (NTC).

**boots**  Leggings worn only by new enlistees in basic training.

**bulkhead**  Wall of a ship.

**carrier**  A large navy ship constructed to carry aircraft and to provide a runway for the taking off and landing of aircraft at sea.

**chit book**   A book of coupons used instead of money to buy things at the Navy Exchange during your training at boot camp.

**Class "A" specialist school**   Technical school for advanced training after boot camp.

**commissary**   Supermarket.

**cruiser**   Type of navy ship.

**Delayed Entry Program**   A program for putting off (delaying) your reporting for active service after you have enlisted.

**deploy**   Ship away from home port.

**destroyer escort**   Type of navy ship.

**ditty bag**   Laundry bag.

**Entrance National Agency Checks (ENTNAC)**   The agency that checks your background to be sure you are not a security risk to the United States.

**E-1, E-2, E-3, up to E-9**   Pay grades. They are the same for all the armed services.

**fireman**   An engineman, machinery repairman or gas turbine systems technician. (NOT a fire fighter!)

**the Fleet**   All ships/boats of the navy make up the Fleet. Also: Group of naval vessels serving in one area under one commander. (Example: the Pacific Fleet.)

**fraternization**   Being friendly with someone.

**frigate**   Type of small navy ship.

**geedunk**   Candy, gum, cafeteria.

**General Orders**   Eleven orders describing duties when standing watch. You must memorize them.

**guidon (pronounced "guide-on")**   Company flag.

**inactive reserve**   After you have finished your active service, you are in the inactive reserve for the time remaining under your enlistment contract. The Delayed Entry Program also places you in the inactive reserve.

**ladder**   Stairs.

**liberty**   Permission granted for you to leave the ship or base for a short time.

**Military Entrance Processing Station (MEPS)**   The place where you take your physical, pass a security check, decide the kind of work you hope to do in the navy, sign the enlistment contract and take the oath.

**Naval Training Center (NTC)**   Where you go through boot camp.

**Navy Exchange (Post Exchange)**   Department store operated by the government.

**noncommissioned officer**   An enlisted sailor from the rank (rating) of petty officer third class on up. (Called "noncom.")

**officer**   A person who has received special training to qualify for a commission, making that person higher in rank than enlisted personnel and noncommissioned officers.

**ordnance**   Bombs, ammunition.

**overhead**   Ceiling.

**Program for Afloat College Education (PACE)**   Courses that may be taken while serving on shipboard.

**rack**   Nickname for bunk.

**rating**   Rank.

**recruit**   Someone who has just joined the navy.

**Recruit Training Command (RTC)**   When you first report for active duty with the navy, you are part of this command.

**recruiter**   Person whose job is to give information about the navy and to enlist persons to serve.

**reveille**   Bugle call for the time to get up in the morning.

**Sea/Air/Mariner Program (SAM)**   A Naval Reserve program.

**seaman**   Sailor; also a rating in the navy.

**Special Warfare Sea, Air and Land (SEAL)**   Specially trained for underwater, land and sea fighting and scouting.

**submarines**   Ships designed for traveling under water.

**taps**   Bugle call for lights out.

**tour of duty**   Term for length of assignment. When your tour is over, you are reassigned to the same place or transferred somewhere else.

**Training and Administration of Reserves (TAR)**   One of the Naval Reserve programs.

# INDEX